Zoom for Begi

The ultimate guide to getting started with Zoom and other conferencing tools for meetings, business video conferences and webinars plus tips and tricks for optimizing your video calls.

By

Marvin Dale

© **Copyright 2020 by Marvin Dale - All rights reserved.**

This document is geared towards providing exact and reliable information in regards to the topic and issue covered. The publication is sold with the idea that the publisher is not required to render accounting, officially permitted, or otherwise, qualified services. If advice is necessary, legal or professional, a practiced individual in the profession should be ordered.

- From a Declaration of Principles which was accepted and approved equally by a Committee of the American Bar Association and a Committee of Publishers and Associations.

In no way is it legal to reproduce, duplicate, or transmit any part of this document in either electronic means or in printed format. Recording of this publication is strictly prohibited and any storage of this document is not allowed unless with written permission from the publisher. All rights reserved.

The information provided herein is stated to be truthful and consistent, in that any liability, in terms of inattention or otherwise, by any usage or abuse of any policies, processes, or directions contained within is the solitary and utter responsibility of the recipient reader. Under no circumstances will any legal responsibility or blame be held against the publisher for any reparation, damages, or monetary loss due to the information herein, either directly or indirectly.

Respective authors own all copyrights not held by the publisher.

The information herein is offered for informational purposes solely, and is universal as so. The presentation of the information is without contract or any type of guarantee assurance.

The trademarks that are used are without any consent, and the publication of the trademark is without permission or backing by the trademark owner.

All trademarks and brands within this book are for clarifying purposes only and are the owned by the owners themselves, not affiliated with this document.

Table of Contents

INTRODUCTION 6

CHAPTER 1: GETTING STARTED WITH ZOOM 8

1.1. Equipment Needed to Use Zoom 15

1.2. Downloading and Installing Zoom 16

1.3. Registration for Zoom 19

1.4. Setting Up a Zoom Meeting 22

1.5. Joining a Zoom Meeting 26

CHAPTER 2: ZOOM VS. OTHER CONFERENCING TOOLS 28

2.1. Zoom Vs. Facebook Rooms 28

2.2. Skype Vs. Zoom 30

2.3. Zoom Vs. Google Hangouts 37

2.4. Microsoft Teams Vs. Zoom 41

2.5. Zoom Vs. ezTalks 46

2.6. Cisco Webex Vs. Zoom 51

2.7. BlueJeans Vs. Zoom 54

CHAPTER 3: TIPS FOR GETTING THE MOST OUT OF ZOOM VIDEO CONFERENCING 59

3.1. Choose Your Surrounding Carefully 60

3.2. Dress for the Occasion 60

3.3. Focus on House Furniture 60

3.4. Invest in a Good Camera 61

3.5. Good Lighting is Important 62

3.6. The Right Posture 62

3.7. Make Eye Contact 62

3.8. Bandwidth Management 63

3.9. Invest in Good Quality Microphones 65

3.10. Make Recurring Meetings With Saved Settings 67

3.11. Record Calls From Zoom as a Video 67

3.12. Record Zoom Meetings on Mobile 68

3.13. Virtual backgrounds 70

3.14. Take Transcripts 71

3.15. Gallery View 72

3.16. Sharing The Screen With Zoom And Using Pause 72

3.17. Zoom Keyboard Shortcuts 73

3.18. Hide Non-Video Participants 73

3.19. Don't Worry (Too Much) 74

CONCLUSION 75

REFERENCES 76

Introduction

Excellent communication is all about making things easier, and who wants to travel to a meeting for hours?

89 percent of remote teams use video conferencing to communicate with colleagues or managers, according to a new survey. The same study explains that about 75 percent of U.S. corporate workers use video communication to work remotely, with a majority showing higher productivity and a stronger work-life balance.

You can say goodbye to Monday's rush hour, corporate attire, and mundane office environments, thanks to communication apps like Zoom. The software for video conferencing allows you to go to work without the need to leave the comfort of your home. It's a response to the latest working-style trend — remote working. Wherever you are, Zoom will ensure all stakeholders can remain on track and work successfully together.

The remote conferencing platform uses cloud computing to invite users to hold online meetings and conferences. It also includes instant messaging, screen sharing, etc. This software offers four different plans that suit your needs best, making it a popular professional online tool.

While many businesses are already using the Zoom video conferencing app for business meetings, interviews, and other purposes, individuals facing long days without contact with friends and family are moving to Zoom for face-to-face and group get-togethers.

Here is a quick guide for those who have not yet tried Zoom, with tips on how to start using its free version. Keep in mind that while one-to-one video calls can go as long as you like, group calls to the Zoom are limited to 40 minutes. You can either opt for Zoom's Pro plan ($14.99 a month) or use an alternative video conferencing service if you want to have long talks without interruption. And additional tips and tricks for using zoom like a Pro, so read below for getting started with zoom.

Chapter 1: Getting Started with Zoom

It is a Video Conferencing service based on the cloud that you can use to meet virtually with others, whether video or audio-only or both while conducting live chats and recording those sessions for viewing later. In 2019 more than half of Fortune 500 companies officially used Zoom.

Usually, when people talk about Zoom, you'll hear the following phrases: Zoom Meeting and Zoom Room. Zoom Meeting refers to a meeting that hosts a video conference using Zoom. You can use a webcam or phone to join these meetings. In the meantime, a Zoom Room is the physical hardware setup that allows companies from their conference rooms to schedule and launch Zoom Meetings.

In addition to a Zoom subscription, Zoom Rooms allow additional subscriptions and are a perfect option for larger companies.

Zoom is also making every effort to provide the highest quality of audio and video during meetings. Indeed, even at meetings with more than 2 people.

Zoom, a forerunner in business video communications, was established to promote and make remote collaboration more secure. This app uses a cloud network to host webinars, tutorials, video calls, and so on. It has been a staple brand in many global businesses since its inception in 2011, including TrendMicro, Logitech, and Uber. It's no surprise, as the platform has been awarded the best product for communication solutions.

Some Core Features of Zoom

- One-on-one meetings: also with the free plan, host unlimited one-on-one sessions.
- Community video conferences: Host up to 500 people (if

you buy the "big group" add-on). The free plan allows you to host up to 40-minute video conferencing and up to 100 participants.

- Sharing the screen: Meet with one-on-one or large groups and share your screen with them to see what you see.

How does the Zoom function?

Zoom offers four separate plans for the users. Their Basic free-of-charge plan features the capacity to host conferences with up to 100 participants simultaneously. The service delivers all the basic features of the Zoom plus an increase in the duration limit from 40 minutes to 24 hours!

There are other features on this package that you can't find in the free edition. Reap the benefits of custom personal meeting ID, 1GB of MP4 or M4A recording, and control of admin feature.

Zoom allows one-to-one chat sessions that can evolve into group calls, internal and external audience training sessions and webinars, and global video meetings of up to 1,000 participants and as many as 49 videos on-screen. The free tier provides for unlimited one-on-one meetings but limits group sessions to 40 minutes and 100 participants. The paid plans begin at $15 per host per month.

Zoom offers four price ranges (not including a subscription to a Zoom Room):

1) **Zoom Unlimited:** Unlimited to this stage. There are an unlimited number of meetings you can hold. Group meetings are capped at 40 minutes in length, with multiple participants, and meetings cannot be recorded.

2) **Zoom Pro:** This tier is costing $14.99/£11.99 per month and host meetings. It allows hosts to create personal IDs for repetitive Zoom Meetings and enables cloud or device recording meetings, but it caps group meeting times at 24

hours.

3) **Business Plan:** This tier costs $19.99/£15.99 per month and host meetings (minimum 10). This helps you mark Zoom meetings with vanity URLs and client logos and provide transcripts of cloud-recorded Zoom meetings and dedicated customer service.

4) **Zoom Enterprise:** This rate costs $19.99/£15.99 per month per meeting host (minimum 100) and is designed for companies with a workforce of 1,000 +. This offers unrestricted cloud video capacity, a client service manager, and webinar and zoom space discounts.

5) **Alternative-Zoom Rooms:** You can sign up for a free 30-day trial if you want to set up Zoom Rooms, after which Zoom Rooms require an additional $49/£39 per month and room rental, while webinars using Zoom cost $40/£32 per month and host.

Zoom Apps

Windows and macOS are available with the desktop app, while Android and iOS have a mobile app.

All these apps allow you to join a meeting without signing in but also let you sign in using a Zoom, Google, Facebook, or SSO account. You can start a meeting from there, join a group, share your screen in a Zoom Room by entering the group ID, start Zoom Meetings, mute / unmute your microphone, invite others to the meeting, start / stop the video, change your screen name, chat in, and start a cloud recording.

You can also start a local recording, live stream your Facebook on Facebook, and create polls, and more if you're a desktop user. In other words, the web version is more fully-featured, but you can still get a lot of mileage from the mobile app if you're a free user.

Zoom Outlook Plugin

As well as the many other applications for the Zoom feature, Zoom can also be used in different ways. There is a Zoom Outlook plugin designed to work directly on your Microsoft Outlook client or as a web-based Add-in to Outlook. This Outlook plug enters the regular Outlook toolbar with a Zoom button and makes a quick click to start or schedule a Zoom meeting.

Browser Extensions for Zoom

The tool for getting a Zoom meeting started or scheduled quickly comes in the form of an extension for your favorite browser. There's an extension to Zoom Chrome and an add-on to Zoom Firefox that allows you to schedule a Zoom meeting through Google Calendar. Just click the Zoom button, and you can start a meeting or schedule one later with all the information about the meeting sent via Google Calendar to make it easy for the participants to join.

Use Zoom on Browser

Joining a Zoom meeting in your browser without the use of the app is relatively tricky. However, it is probable. For example, you can directly enter a meeting by using a Zoom Web client connection that looks like this — zoom.us/wc/join/your-meeting-id.

A browser extension has also been worked out by some clever bods that let you enter a meeting straight from your browser without the app's hassle. This is perfect if, for example, you are on a protected work laptop that doesn't require you to install any software.

Zoom deliberately hides the link "join from your browser," so here's a small browser extension (20 lines) that redirects Zoom links transparently to use their web client:

Zoom-Redirector

https:/twitter.com/rowan m/status/1241693796229931008 ...

Zoom Redirector is a browser extension that redirects any meeting links to use the browser-based web client transparently.

Zoom Retriever

Use: https:/zoom.us/wc/{your-meeting-id}/start to go straight to the web-version of a zoom meeting. (No app or extension needed)

https:/twitter.com/Ouren/status124139818181205889024

This link is available for Firefox and Chrome right now. Although it's worth noting that Zoom isn't officially produced.

It is possible to get Zoom to work on your TV, and you can have a full-screen video call.

What is the difference between free Zoom and paid Zoom?

There are a couple of variations worth mentioning between the paid and free Zoom plans.

Free Users

You can install the Zoom app to your computer or phone, and join any meeting with a meeting ID provided. You can also opt to deactivate audio or video before joining. By linking your account to Google, you could even create your free Zoom account, and from there, you can host a new meeting, schedule a meeting, join a meeting, share a screen, add contacts, etc.

Just keep in mind that one computer, one tablet and one phone at a time can only sign in to Zoom. Zoom said you'd automatically log out on the first device if you sign in to an additional device while logging in to another device of the same type.

Paid Users

If your system administrator has a Pro, Company, or Enterprise account, you can sign up and download Zoom to your device using your Work Address. Then you want to synchronize Zoom with your calendar so that you can schedule Zoom meetings and invite remote participants to join.

If you set up a Zoom Room, you'll need a computer to synchronize and run Zoom Meetings, and a tablet for the Zoom Meetings to launch. You will also need a microphone, camera, and speaker, at least one HDTV monitor to view participants from remote meetings, and an HDMI cable to share computer screens on display and an internet cable to connect to you.

You will also need to download "Zoom Rooms for Conference Room" for the tablet in the meeting room on the in-room computer, and "Zoom Room Controller." Then you can synchronize those rooms with the shared calendar of your company so that employees can see which meeting rooms are available.

Security Issues and Updates of Zoom

A variety of questions about Zoom have recently been raised, both in terms of security and issues with unwelcome visitors known as Zoombombers.

The company has made numerous steps to combat these issues and reassure consumers that security and privacy are relevant. This involves easy things like deleting the meet ID from the title bar of the call, so if users share online screenshots, the meeting won't be exposed to future misuse.

What are Zoombombers?

Zoom's rise in popularity will lead the company to be exploited by Internet trolls and people who have too much time on their hands. Some people have been hunting down public and unsafe Zoom meetings and letting themselves in, then "bombing" with graphic videos, pornography, and other inappropriate content on the call.

Here is a guide about how to avoid Zoombombing, and there are various ways you can stop this from happening, including protecting your calls, preventing screen sharing, and even disabling footage. The team behind Zoom is also doing daily updates to keep your calls safe and stable.

Default Security Updates

To help reassure users, the Zoom has been updated with several security changes. Several of which was the provision for Zoom meetings to have a password as usual. Combined with virtual waiting rooms, this means that in reality, only those people who have been invited to the call are allowed in. Another phase in ensuring all calls are safe and stable.

Security Tools Of Zoom

Zoom has also made it easy to organize your meetings and to protect them when they happen. There are a range of security options that you can now access with a few taps. This includes the opportunity to lock the meeting when it begins so that no new people can enter, delete current call participants, mutate participants, and even disable private chat.

To access the Zoom protection tools, you can simply press the protection button that appears in the window when the call happens, or swing over a participant to connect with them directly - for example, to delete them from the call.

Reporting other Participants of Meeting

It is now possible to report the participants who are not invited or who cause trouble. Now you can submit a report to the Zoom Confidence and Safety team to deal with device misuse, along with removing them from the call. For the future, this would help block them from the service and interfere with specific calls.

To do this, click on the meeting seat button and then press submit.

1.1. Equipment Needed to Use Zoom

You will need to use the videoconferencing feature Zoom:

- A laptop, mobile, smartphone, or tablet computer.
- An Internet Explorer
- Speakers, a microphone, and a camera mounted or connected to your monitor or your mobile device.
- Network Desktop, Mac, Linux, and Mobile Computer Specifications

You'll benefit from having: A set of built-in microphone headphones, which can be attached to your computer or mobile device. Those may be headphones (hand buds) in-ear or headphones over the hand. The microphone may be inserted into the wire or placed on a boom. Capable of wired or wireless headphones.

It is suggested using a pair of headphones with a microphone attached, as they will give you:

- Listening fast
- Speak clarification
- Less background noise for all delegates

Such types of headphones have a microphone. If you don't have a set of microphones included, you can use a pair of headphones without an integrated microphone, and use the microphone built into your computer or mobile device.

You may use the speakers and microphones built into your

computer or mobile device when you don't have headphones or a microphone.

1.2. Downloading and Installing Zoom

Download the Mobile app

What if you're on the go and need to host a short video meeting with several smartphone users? If anyone has a Google+ account, you might use Google+ Hangouts —. If not, you can try Cloud Meetings on ZOOM. This easy to use tool allows you to host screen sharing meetings or regular video meetings.

Zoom is a service that includes a robust Android app and allows free hosting of 40-minute meetings for up to 25 attendees. If you need larger meetings or more extended, check out the price plan for the Zoom. But, the free plan is great for those who need smaller meetings.

The use of the Zoom has one caveat. The service is exclusively for Windows and Mac on the desktop (not even Chromebooks get to enjoy the Zoom experience). However, if you're on the go your Android platform will be just fine — and it's incredibly simple to start/join a meeting.

You'll want to hop over to the Zoom website and sign up for an account before using ZOOM Cloud Meetings. It's time to install the app once you've completed that and to invite people to meetings. Either a compatible mobile platform or the Android app installed on their Android smartphone or tablet will be needed for anyone you invite to a meeting.

Installing the Software

To install a smartphone app with IOS or Android, do the following:

- Open App Store on your Apple or Android device.

- Look for ZOOM Cloud Meetings

- Locate and tap zoom.us for entry
- Press Install button
- View the List of permissions
- If the listing of permissions is appropriate tap Agree
- Let the installation end.
- When enabled, you'll find the launcher either on the home screen or on the (or both) device drawer. Click the key, then log into your account with ZOOM Cloud Meetings.

Download Zoom on PC

With more people starting to work in most sectors from home, remote conferencing technology has never been more relevant. Services such as Zoom, which offer online meetings and video calls, become more critical than ever to help businesses run smoothly while physical offices are closed.

Fortunately, installing Zoom to your PC is a quick process that will get you up and running in just a few minutes with the service. While you will need to sign up for a free account to use zoom, you'll be able to use it immediately once the program is installed on your computer.

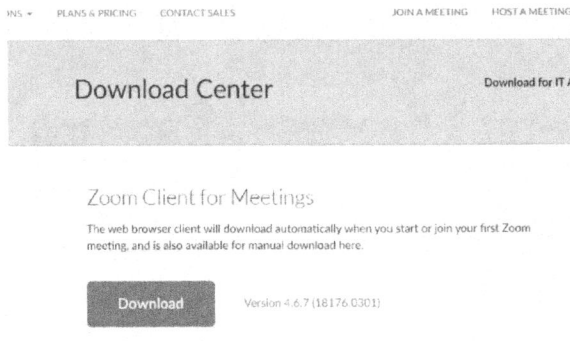

Here is how you can download Zoom to your PC.

1. Open the internet browser on your computer, and link to the Zoom.us website.

2. Scroll down to the bottom of the page, and in the footer of the web page, click "Download."

3. Click "Download" on the Download Center page under the section called "Zoom Client for Meetings."

4. You will then start installing the Zoom app. To begin the installation process, you can then click on the .exe file.

When enabled, you'll need to log into your Zoom account, which can be set up via the Zoom website if you don't have one already. If developed, you can use Zoom to meet all your video calls and online needs as usual.

1.3. Registration for Zoom

Of course, the primary step to do is to register for the service. You can do that either from your cell phone or from your laptop.

Next, you should cover the Internet service.

1. Go to the Sign-Up page for Zoom. You will be given a few options to create an account. You should type your e-mail in the "Your Work E-mail Address" box at the top. When you do so, proceed to phase two. Even though Zoom asks for a work e-mail, a personal e-mail will work fine. Still, you should be aware that there have been reports of Zoom leaking some e-mail addresses and user images via Zoom's Contact Directory because the app may assume that people with certain e-mail domains work for the same business. Nonetheless, from automatically appearing in that directory, Zoom blacklists some common e-mail domains such as gmail.com and yahoo.com.

2. An account is also created by clicking on the buttons "Sign in with Google" or "Sign in with Facebook," after which you will simply download the Zoom desktop app and proceed to step 7.

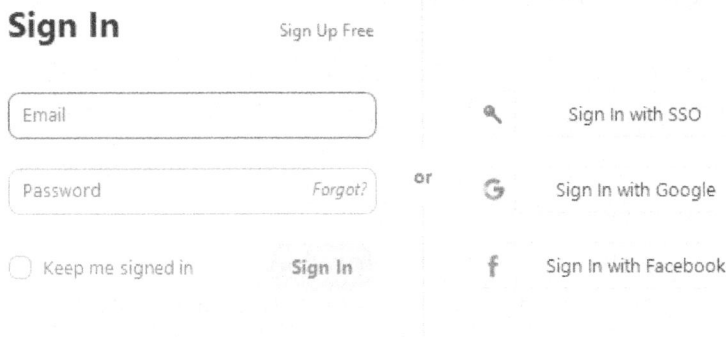

3. When you have entered an e-mail, Zoom will send an e-mail to that address for activation. To activate your account, click the "Activate Account" button in the e-mail or copy and paste the activation URL in your browser.

4. Enter the details that appear, your first and last name, and a password, on your web browser page.

5. You may invite other people on the next page to create a free Zoom account via e-mail. If you wish, you can skip the move.

6. You will then be given a link to your personal meeting URL, and you will have the option to press the "Start Meeting Now" orange button to start a test meeting. You should be asked to download the Zoom desktop app when you copy that URL into your browser or click that orange button. To install the program, obey the prompts.

7. After installing the Zoom app, you will see "Join a Meeting" or "Sign In" buttons. Click "Sign In" to start your Test Meeting.

8. On the next page, enter your browser's e-mail and

20

password that you just used to register for Zoom. If you registered using the buttons "Login with Google" or "Login with Facebook" then press those buttons here and follow the prompts.

9. Make sure you're on the "Back" tab once you've signed in, then press the "New Meeting" orange button in the Zoom app. Your meeting is set to begin.

Logging in through Mobile app

If you use the Mobile App to sign up for zoom, it is similar to how it's on the Internet.

1. Download the Android or iOS app. You'll be given the options for joining a meeting, signing up for Zoom, or signing in to a Zoom account when you open the app. Tap the "Register" button.

2. On the next page, you'll be asked to enter your first and last name e-mail address and check a box to agree to Zoom's terms of service. Tap "Sign Up" after you do so, and you will receive an activation e-mail.

3. Tap the "Activate Account" button in the e-mail you receive or copy the activation URL to your mobile browser and paste it.

4. From there, to make an account, you'll be asked to complete the same steps outlined above, just from your mobile browser.

5. Once you have reached the screen with your personal Zoom Meeting URL and orange "Start Meeting Now" button, tap either, and you will be taken directly to the waiting room in the Zoom app for your test meeting.

6. Click the "Sign In" button at the bottom of the screen for the meeting to open. Type your login information on the next page and press the "Sign In" button.

7. Your test meeting is scheduled to open in the app.

1.4. Setting Up a Zoom Meeting

To learn how to host or schedule the meeting from inside Zoom.us code, follow the steps mentioned below.

Step # 1:

Open application Zoom.us.

Whether you want to host the next meeting or schedule a later meeting, go to one of the following sections:

- Host a Conference
- Time-up a meeting

Step # 2:

Host a Conference

Depending on your needs, either press Start without Video or Start with a Video button.

Step # 3:

Press the Invite button that appears at the bottom of the page.

Step # 4

The invitation can be exchanged in a few different ways:

- Clicking the Copy URL button, then paste the URL to the participants you wish to invite in an e-mail message.
- Click the Invitation to Copy button and then paste the message into an e-mail to the participants you would like to invite.
- Click one of the buttons on the e-mail service. The e-mail service you selected will appear with a pre-formatted invitation.

Step # 5

- Schedule a Meeting
- Click the Timing button.

Step # 6

- Enter the title of a meeting in the Topic area.

Step # 7

In the options When, enter:

Starting Time

Duration (45 minutes for Basic accounts only allowed)

Timing Zone

Step # 8

Choose from the options below:

Audio: Tel., VoIP Only or Both

Step # 9

If desired, select additional Meeting Options, including require password for the meeting.

Step # 10

Select what form of the calendar you wish to use to build the invitation.

* Note: You can copy and paste the meeting information into any calendar program by selecting Other Calendars.

Step # 11

Click the Timing button.

Step # 12

Your meeting is scheduled to take place.

To invite other members, press the Copy button to clipboard and then paste the details into your preferred calendar program.

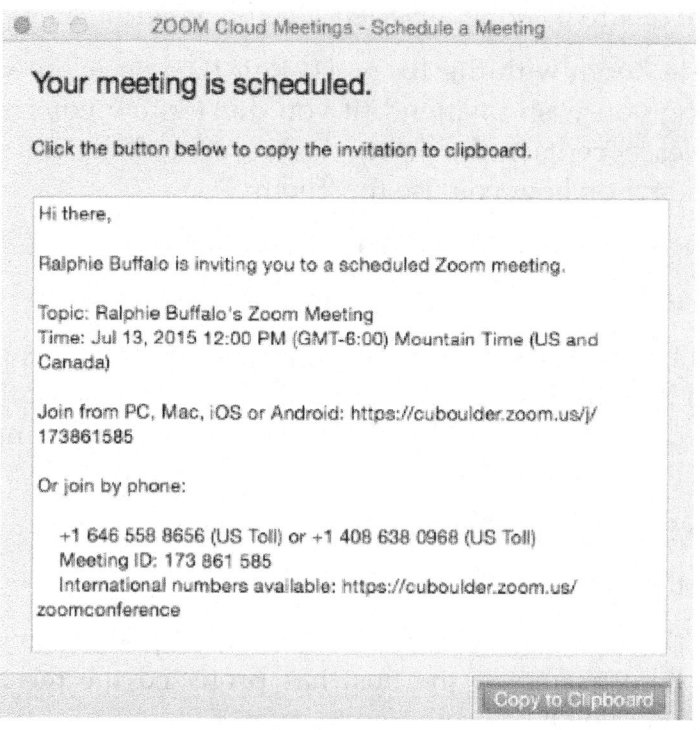

1.5. Joining a Zoom Meeting

Sign in to your account on Zoom.

Although it is possible to join a Zoom meeting as a guest, it is recommended that you sign with your IU account to zoom for a more secure meeting experience before entering a meeting.

Provide Zoom with the 10- or 11-digit ID associated with the meeting you wish to attend (if you don't know your meeting ID, please contact the host). Follow the directions below, depending on how you use the Zoom:

Through a Browser (like Google Chrome):

Browse to https:/iu.zoom.us/j/meeting ID.

You'll be prompted to start the application Zoom. You will be joined in with the meeting once you open the form. If the host has protected the meeting by password, you'll be prompted to enter it.

Zoom Desktop Applications:

Open the app to zoom in, and click Join.

Type the ID of the meeting and set the options for joining. Click here to Join. If the host has protected the meeting by password, you'll be prompted to enter it.

Zoom Mobile Application IOS or Android:

Open the App for Zoom, and tap Join.

If you see the "Join a Meeting" option, you must sign in to your IU account at your Zoom.

Enter the ID of the meeting and set your options for joining. Tap on Meeting Join. If the host has protected the meeting by password, you'll be prompted to enter it.

Chapter 2: Zoom Vs. Other Conferencing Tools

For remote teams, the most preferred collaboration devices are the Zoom, Skype, Facebook rooms, Google Hangouts, Microsoft Teams, ezTalks, Cisco Webex, and BlueJeans etc.

All of these platforms can be used to hold video calls, chat, and host meetings or webinars. And if you're looking for a new platform to help you do these things, you're probably considering platforms like these.

Ultimately, the variations between all of them may not seem significant. But the decision to implement one over another can still impact your team significantly. It's easy to say from the experiences of a remote team that every platform fits different needs, and that is why it is important to your decision to understand the pros and cons, features and pricing, etc.

2.1. Zoom Vs. Facebook Rooms

Since Facebook Messenger Rooms and Zoom are end-of-the-day video calling applications, we compared them both based on their functionality, availability, and more.

Since Facebook Messenger Rooms and Zoom are end-of-the-day video calling applications, we compared them both based on their functionality, availability, and more.

Facebook has finally revealed what its Zoom competitor, Messenger Quarters, can be renamed.

The video calling application is integrated into the standalone Facebook Messenger app and is intended for personal use. In comparison, Zoom is based on technical video conferencing.

But since both are end-of-day video calling apps, here is a comparison based on functionality, quality of the web, and more.

1) Availability

Both are present in iOS and android when it comes to availability, and have a web edition that can be obtained from anywhere. This means you can reach it on Windows OS, as well as on macros and ChromeOS. What's more, you don't have to download a separate Messenger Rooms app, as it's built into the Messenger app itself.

2) Free or Not

One of the most significant benefits for the Facebook Messenger Room here is that it's cost-free. Yeah, you do not have to pay for any of the features in Zoom as you do. While Zoom also has a free tier, most of its features are restricted to the paid edition. Zoom has three paid plans costing $14.99 a month, and $19.99 a month. However, up to 100 participants are still in favor of the free version.

3) Characteristics

In this one, Zoom gets an edge as the video conferencing application can support up to 100 participants in one call session. The paid version can support up to 350: participants, and even 500. However, at the moment, Facebook Messenger Rooms are limited to 50 participants.

Yet when it comes to video call size, Messenger Rooms is taking the lead. It allows you to speak with 50 people for unlimited minutes at a time, whereas Zoom's free tier can support 100 (or less) participants in a 40-minute call. The paid version can tolerate calls up to 24 hours.

Since Zoom is designed for organizational use, it also has the function of call recording, and something is missing from Messenger Room right now.

The biggest advantage of Facebook is the audience that it already has in the main app and the Messenger app. Using News Feed, Groups, and Events, you can start and share rooms on Facebook, and it's comfortable for people to drop by.

Facebook says it will quickly add ways to create Instagram Direct, WhatsApp, and Portal rooms. Though both offer you the versatility to communicate text during a video call and share screens with others.

2.2. Skype Vs. Zoom

Several applications for video conferencing are on the market. Skype is among the competition's largest and oldest brands. It allows single-to-one video calls, instant messaging, screen sharing, group calls, and file sharing, much like Zoom.

Skype redirects messages to an email inbox for those who participate offline. Skype is still lagging behind its competition, though, in that the platform only allows up to ten participants at a time. A no-go definitely to larger conferences.

According to Global Industry Forecasts, video conferencing is expected to become a 20-million-dollar industry by the end of 2024. With this growth, there are hundreds of platforms to choose from; Zoom vs. Skype is just one of the companies' most popular debates.

Below is a comparison of Zoom vs. Skype's features, pricing, and product performance to secure the best video conferencing needs.

Overview Zoom vs. Skype

Zoom

It's an innovative cloud-based with modern conference tools.

Zoom derives with breakout sessions that can be used to divide your viewers (e.g., customers or employees) into small groups for like webinar training, specific topics, or some online class discussions.

The organizer has the power to monitor the meeting to the full with Zoom. You can also mute all microphones when not in use, monitor presentation access for the attendants, and so on. Besides, this method allows the participants to participate by digitally raising their hands to the discussion.

The chat utility of Zoom also allows viewers to communicate directly with your instructor and with other participants, thus ensuring a collective classroom setup.

Skype

Imagine communicating with your employees directly from your PC / phone through instant short messaging service, screen sharing, file sharing, and informal or formal audio or video calls. Effective and direct, that's all about Skype.

Skype is designed to make simple communication using revolutionary technology. It intuitive chat interface, like Zoom, allows users to send prompt messages to other users. Users can integrate video with audio from their chat windows without any effort.

General Information

When considering Skype vs. Zoom, the biggest challenge is that they are both very powerful channels of communication. Deciding between these two can be difficult, as both are efficient and cost-effective.

By definition, a Zoom is a software-based on video or audio conferencing that was intended to promote collaboration through an advanced integrated system with featuring web conferences, group messaging, and important online meetings.

On the opposite hand, Skype provides powerful tools for text, voice, and video, providing users with a smart way to share the experiences with others, no matter where they are.

1) **Devices**

Zoom supports Web platforms such as Android, iPhone, Mac, iPad.

Web-based Skype supports all Windows, Android, and iPhones.

Zoom is filled with a variety of features, including video conferences , streamlined scheduling, and collaboration between groups. This platform's other powerful features include local and cloud recording in premium audio feature, and in Zoom Meetings and Zoom Rooms.

Skype also comes with powerful chat tools, including Skype-to-Skype calls, community calls, call-forwards, one-to-one video calls, and instant messaging. You can send and exchange emails, video messages, displays, files, and contacts.

2) **Clients**

Zoom and Skype both deliver premium video conferencing solutions — a factor they have loyal customers around the globe. Zoom boasts loyal customers such as Washington University, UBER, and Zendesk, while Skype is the choice of VerbalizeIt, AIRDEX, and Diverse Learners.

3) **Designed for**

Both Zoom and Skype are perfect for the small businesses to significant business, but freelancers are also popular with Skype's free plan.

4) Pricing

Zoom offers four pricing packages for enterprises: Zoom Basic Plan, Zoom Pro Plan, Zoom Business Plan, and Zoom Enterprise Plan.

Basic Plan

The basic package — which is explicitly tailored for personal meetings — is free, can host up to 100 people, and provides one-on-one sessions without restrictions. It's an excellent gratuitous bid. You will use this program to:

- Team of conducts meets for up to forty minutes
- Have a plethora of meetings
- Get the support online
- Enjoy the functions of web and video conferencing
- Make sure community collaboration is safe

Zoom Pro Plan

It is for the small teams, and it costs $14.99 per user per month. It comes with all the basic plan functionality and can accommodate 100 participants. You'll get unlimited meeting duration with the Zoom Pro Plan, assigned custom personal meeting ID, assigned scheduler and reporting meetings.

This program also includes business interoperability user management tools, admin controls, REST API, and Skype. Users can store and share large amounts of data with 1GB data of mp4 and m4a Cloud recording.

The optional Zoom add-on plans

This include five sub-plans:

- $40 a month for extra cloud recording storage.
- $49 per month for 323/ SIP Room Connector.
- $49 a month for joining Zoom Rooms.

- $100 a month for toll-free dialing / Call Me.
- $40 a month for adding video webinars.

Business Plan

The business strategy for the zoom, which is worth $19.99 a month per user, is limited to smaller businesses. Equipped with all of the Pro plan's functionality, mid-sized companies will use it to take their connectivity to another level.

The plan lets you host up to 10 hosts, it has an admin control dashboard, telephone support, and a vanity URL. The Business Plan is an excellent option if you prefer on-premise placement than certain characteristics of the scheme include:

- **Manage domains and one-way sign-on**
- **Client branding and customized emails**
- **Integration with LTI**

Zoom Plan For Enterprise

Zoom Enterprise is for $19.99 per person/host per month. In this plan, which includes all of the Business Plan features which needs you to have a minimum of 100 hosts. Up to 200 participants are allowed into this plan.

The Enterprise package is ideal for large organizations with diverse meeting needs, with unrestricted cloud storage, a zealous client service manager, and executive company feedback.

Skype

Skype is free of charge. However, if you're looking to improve efficiency and increase revenue, Skype has a $2-per-month enterprise price package per user.

Business Plan

For Skype's Business Plan, users can use solid authentication as well as encryption to enjoy features like online meetings (250 participants) and secure communication lines.

Online Plan 2

This plan costs $5.50 a month per user and is designed for online business meetings. You can use Online Plan 2 to:

- Join any Equipment
- Enjoy HD video in the group as well as audio calling (for 250 people)
- Receive mobile technical assistance at the client level
- Office versions available online
- 50 GB Postbox
- 1 TB Store File

Office 365 Professional Premium

This plan is for $12.50 per user per month. The Office 365 Company Critical plan has notable features, including:

- Government software pre-installed on PC / Mac
- Tablet and mobile apps
- In addition, Microsoft's parent company Skype has supported Microsoft Teams over Skype as a forum for meeting and video conferencing. As a result, Skype support may diminish in favor of Teams over time.

Backend Integrations Zoom

Zoom supports

- Microsoft One Drive
- Salesforce Box
- Slack
- Okta
- Microsoft Outlook
- LTI (Canvas, Desire2Learn, Backboard and Moodle)
- Google Chrome
- Marketo
- Facebook Centrify
- Intel Unite
- Kubi
- Zapier
- RSA

Other integrations that Zoom supports include:
- Google Drive, DropBox, Pardot
- Firefox and Acuity Calendar
- Eloqua and the Microsoft Active Directory
- Hipchat, Infusionsoft, and HubSpot

Skype

Provides integration with such programs as:
- Office (Word, Lync, Outlook, PowerPoint)
- WordPress
- Mendix
- Lucid Meetings
- OnePage CRM

- Bitium
- Cayzu Helpdesk
- BigContacts
- SalesExec
- Interactive Intelligence CaaaS
- 1CRM
- Grasshopper
- Slack
- GroupWise

Skype can also be integrated with other systems, such as:

- CRM Agile
- Wimi and 88 Center for Virtual Touch
- Microsoft Dynamics Online CRM
- The Concierge and Yugma Moxie
- Zoom vs. Skype: The Low Line

Zoom and Skype both deliver customized solutions and are designed to take interactions from your company to the next level. But the free and paid third-party enhancements apps enhance Zoom and give it a slight edge.

2.3. Zoom Vs. Google Hangouts

In 2013, Google Hangouts was released as a way to merge previously separate apps from the company, such as Google Talk (for calls), Google+ Messenger (for chat), and the original Google+ Hangout (for video) into one. Over time, the platform has added voice calling and video calling to accommodate all types of virtual conversation.

Zoom was released the same year, but in 2017, according to The Business Journals, it started climbing up app charts. It has since gained traction — especially during the recent outbreak, when many people turn to the app for their (professional or personal) video conferencing needs, according to CNBC. Reuters reports that since January, the app has increased its daily active user base by 67 percent.

Although both channels are useful at the core to stay linked during these social distancing and self-quarantining times, some main features make them separated.

Whether you like to use a video chat app to hold work meetings or stay up-to-date on the latest gossip from your friends, here are the most noticeable differences between Google Hangouts and Zoom.

1) **Number of Participants**

The number of people a video conference app allows you to have in one meeting could be a make-or-break point for you, depending on whether you want to have huge company-wide meetings (or are just super-popular).

Google Hangouts allows up to 160 people to chat but limits its video calls to only 25 persons per call (with the 10 most active participants shown at the bottom of the screen). This works for those who have meetings in small groups or just want to chat with some friends.

By contrast, Zoom allows users to have a video call with up to 100 participants. The Gallery View feature lets you see on one screen up to 49 of those participants. Plus, if you want an even bigger meeting, you can have up to 500 people (as long as you get the $ 50-month Large Meeting add-on).

2) Price

If you're only searching for a video-conferencing device for friends and personal use, you may want to invest as close to nothing as you can.

If you only want to use Google Hangouts to make and receive phone and video calls, you can do this at no charge. But, if you wish to storage to keep records of your meetings and calls, pricing for 30 GB of storage starts at $6 per month.

Zoom has various packages, priced depending on how many features are included. The free choice allows you to have your meetings unlimited and up to 100 people. You pay $14.99 a month for a pro account (meaning for small teams) per host.

3) Additional Characteristics

Not everybody is using video-conferencing software for video calls only. Often, it's good to learn that your apps can do more.

If you're searching for something a little easier, then your best bet is Google Hangouts. The software does have additional features, but most do not require extra practice. These include group conferencing, intelligent changeover, and integration with other Google apps. Most of the time, you can only log into and start using Google Hangouts.

At first, zoom may seem a little more complicated, but it provides a great set of additional features if you'd like some fun. They provide a note-taking annotation tool, an automated transcript-creator, and even a touch-up feature.

4) Capabilities of Screen Sharing

Whether you're in a coworker meeting or talking to friends about that strange thing your cat did when no one was looking, you sometimes need visual aids.

And if you're already on a video call, this is where the applications for screen sharing come in. Google Hangouts allows you to share your computer in the video call with others, but it is bounded to one user at a time.

By contrast, Zoom allows multiple people to share their screens at once within meetings.

5) GIFs & Emojis

This may not be the most prominent feature you're looking for, but sometimes your messages just need a little more fun. While this feature is more for those who talk with friends, you never know when you want to give a cool "thumbs up" emoji to your boss.

Google Hangouts lets you search and use a wide range of emojis (animated as well as unanimous) and GIFs. You can throw them into chats whenever you wish.

Although Zoom does not let you use emojis, it does allow you to use GIFs. Plus, it will enable admins to turn on and off the skill. This could be useful during meetings which should be all-business. But even so, you can still use the whiteboard capabilities of Zoom to draw on various slides and screens, so there is a way to get around that.

6) Time Limit

When you are searching for a video conferencing device for work meetings, the time limit for video chatting may not matter as much. However, if your video-app-related activities consist of being on call at all hours of the day with your best friends, time limits might be a breaker in the deal.

Google Hangouts has no known limitations regarding the length of calls you can make to others. Nevertheless, Zoom has a limit for those using its free package.

And though you can make infinite numbers of calls, each call will last only up to 40 minutes. If you use a pro account, or anything more expensive than that, the limit will move up to 24 hours.

Aside from learning about the features of an app, often it just takes you to use it and compare it to others firsthand to find out which choice is better for you. Happy chatting anyway!

2.4. Microsoft Teams Vs. Zoom

Which is better with Microsoft Teams vs. Zoom? As the UC market is moving gradually from UC to UCaaS, the main competitive scenario that most customers are debating with us is no longer Skype for Business vs. Cisco, but the cloud scenario (which now involves both video conferencing and audio, with a start (Zoom Phone functionality) of Zoom vs. Microsoft Teams in the cloud, and when it comes to comparing Microsoft Teams vs. Zoom, the solution is just as tricky in the modern UCaaS environment now as it was in the old battle between Microsoft and Cisco.

Over the last couple of years, each of these relatively new platforms has seen rapid development, accumulating an impressive number of features and fans. Don't blink, the ongoing competition, creation, and fulfillment of new scenarios for end-user and enterprise fulfillment are likely to be rapid-fire over at least the next few years.

Many companies are currently in the Skype for Business mix. Still, with the recent announcement of the end-of-life date for Skype for Business Online (and speculation that the on-prem edition would have a similar fate), it is prompting many IT teams to resolve what their next step will be for their ecosystem of connectivity and cooperation.

So how do you decide between Zoom and Microsoft Teams? First, look at the break down of each platform and then dive in to equate them as close as we can to a level playing field.

Zoom

Zoom is a pioneer (and potentially the pack's highest-profile since its April IPO) in the video communications industry, addressing digital communications at all endpoints through their cloud platform for video, audio conferencing, collaboration, chatting, and webinars.

What are Microsoft Teams like?

Microsoft Teams is the all-encompassing work stream collaboration with Microsoft plus a centralized communications platform – connecting meetings, calls, chats, and file sharing with the Office 365 application stack to bring everyone together in a shared workspace.

Breakdown of the Microsoft Teams Vs. Zoom

Microsoft Teams and Zoom both converge and compete at a very high level by providing a range of video conferencing tools (including room systems) and UC telephony services. Drilling more in-depth into the more complex functionality, Usability, pricing, and alignment is how companies can determine trade-offs and make the right decisions as to which platform is the match.

1) Characteristics

Where apps are concerned, both Zoom and Teams allow online meetings, conversations, calls, screen sharing, and file sharing. Microsoft's collaboration of Teams and its Office 365 platform is the difference between the two. This makes it possible for Microsoft Teams to be a one-stop-shop for many organizations.

This also allows seamless collaboration, backups, and the search for files.

But going some way to complement the incorporation of Microsoft's Office365, Zoom and Slack features a wide-ranging relationship and a collection of technological combinations.

Zoom, as an organization, is a much newer organization than Microsoft's behemoth. Yet, it leads to competing with its aggressive roadmap, and because it doesn't have to worry about managing (and eventually leaving) a set of legacy customers at the premises.

2) UX (Utility Interface)

In Microsoft Teams vs. Zoom debate, the user interface and experience are genuinely where Zoom excels. Zoom users are all raving about its simple interface and the ability to get end users up and running with limited to no training or IT support.

Microsoft Teams face a bigger challenge as users need to get to grips with how to communicate in various networks and teams, integrate file sharing, as well as the other Office 365 apps built into teams. Although the full range of interactive work stream features built into Teams obviously enables it to give a wider field of use and scenarios (and therefore a greater value) than Zoom, this specific scope is also, in certain respects, its Achilles heel as regards aboard.

3) Room Systems

When areas of the arena Zoom vs. Teams continue to become highly commoditized, one field of unique distinction is the "space systems" that are built within an enterprise.

A room layout can range from a basic configuration of the huddle room to a deluxe conference room for executives. Although both provide app control, touch upgrades, mobile companion interactions, and dual-screen room support, Zoom has the added advantage of counting people, and Teams have proximity detection. Another distinction between Zoom and Microsoft Teams is that Zoom certifies all integrators and hardware suppliers while only the hardware solutions are approved by Teams.

4) Pricing

Microsoft Teams and Zoom offer each a free version of the platform, offering more advanced features with paid plans.

Microsoft Teams Free version includes restricted chat and collaboration, apps, and services for productivity, meetings, and calls, and security. Two large pieces that are missing with the free version include administration tools or support from Microsoft.

The free version of Zoom includes meetings that can host up to 100 participants (with a group meeting limit of 40 minutes), unlimited 1:1 meetings, online support, video and web conferencing features, group collaboration features, and security.

Microsoft's Premium plan is marginally cheaper per user than the equivalent Pro plan for Zoom, but they are priced equally with their corporate plans.

5) UC Telephony

The ability to make calls at an enterprise level is crucial, especially for video, audio, conferencing, and messaging business communications. This type of feature has initially been a stronghold of Microsoft, as Zoom did not initially have a phone system product.

The Zoom Telephone is the enterprise voice response. The modern and rapidly maturing cloud phone system offers smart call routing and management, auto-attendant / IVR, interoperability with conventional endpoints like voicemail, call history, caller ID and mobile dialing, plus call recording. As with Microsoft Teams, it offers the software on both desktop and mobile devices. Furthermore, Zoom's "Bring Your Own Carrier" system is a direct response to the Direct Routing function of Teams, enabling Zoom Phone organizations to use established PSTN service providers in many world markets.

6) Zoom Debate

The biggest win for Microsoft Teams is its tight, baked-in integration with Office 365 applications. Still, beyond that, Microsoft Teams have more than 70 combinations that include ticket management options, polls, weather, news, etc.

Integrations, usually, in the case of Microsoft, are to put user data into its network. On the flip side, the Zoom is often added to other platforms as an integration. One great example of this is how Slack and Zoom work collectively. In addition to the Slack combination, Zoom has more than 100 combinations, including an Office 365 integration.

Zoom and Teams: If you are considering both systems running simultaneously, you would need a common management framework that works for both. It is just that PowerSuite does!

In reality, on both Teams and Zoom, we are increasingly seeing large companies choosing to "standardize." Microsoft Teams are excellent for internal collaboration, whereas Zoom is often preferred for external work, with customers or with guest vendors. Since they communicate with one another, it is simple for users to build specific scenarios in which to use when.

Multiplatform in the new digital workforce is becoming ever more the current standard. A study found in a recent survey that 85 percent of users use multiple platforms for collaborative apps.

2.5. Zoom Vs. ezTalks

The ezTalks Cloud Meeting is another neck-to-neck rivalry from Zoom. All apps boast, such as an infinite number of user sessions, high-definition audio, and video access. Both allow users to hold conferences that have as many as 100 at a time. Screen sharing and recording meetings are some of this program's other features. ezTalk also has a whiteboard and co-annotation interactive tools that Zoom just doesn't do

Nowadays, more and more business owners can accept Online Meeting in their day-to-day business work because it overcomes geographical and time barriers, enabling people from various regions/countries to hold or attend a meeting without any constraint simultaneously. This advance is accessible thanks to some program that provides online meeting solutions. Remarkably, ezTalks and Zoom are the two best video conferencing applications for these features. But there is a highly contentious topic connected with one being the right aid to hold a conference.

What is ezTalks?

ezTalks, a versatile cloud-based HD video conferencing software that features a fresh-looking user interface, leads to successful and seamless online education, online training, online meetings, online webinars, and online presentations anywhere, anywhere.

It was widely used by all industries, such as industry, government, education, training, healthcare, legal, etc.

The developers also offer a server version, in addition to the standard free version of ezTalks, for any company or organization to deploy on their own network. Even if you don't have any prior knowledge of using any such tools, ezTalks with integrated hardware & software can make the entire process completely simple and awesome.

Comparison ezTalks vs. Zoom:

1) Features:

The resource you select will help the team with the procedures, workflows, reports, and needs that matter. When it comes to this, its features & functionality are important to consider. Then, based on some prominent features, here is a comparison of ezTalks with Zoom.

ezTalks:

- **Group / Private high-quality video & audio;**
- **Taping & Playback;**
- **All-in-one Huddle Room video conferencing equipment;**
- **Used on universal system platforms like iOS and Android;**
- **Lots of built-in add-ons;**
- **Secure, and best sharing of screens;**
- **Supported dial-in phone service;**
- **Control room management system for high-class meeting**
- **Safety and encryption;**

Zoom:

- **Sharing of web displays, community networking, and appearance at the same time;**

- Integration of H.323 / SIP in-room system;
- MPEG 4 Client recording and recording in the cloud;
- Remarks and co-annotation;
- Encryption of a secure Socket Layer (SSL);
- Broadcast to YouTube or Facebook;
- Virtual backdrop;
- Cloud Recording & Playback.

2) Pros & Cons

Though both are outstanding software for video conferencing with common aspects, they still have their respective strengths and weakness.

ezTalks:

Pros

- Safe to use & web
- Safety (Onetime Password)
- As extensive as room for meeting
- Private and group chat in real-time, informal discussion and sharing, useful recording, and playback.
- Seamless Desktop and Mobile Meeting (Windows, Mac, iOS, devices based on Android)
- Must only link to the Internet

Cons

- No available API

Zoom:

Pros

- Fast to set up (approx. 3s from download to install)

- Unlimited tier (up to 100 delegates)
- Specific Industry plans
- Personal meeting ID customized.
- Unlimited duration for meetings of all sizes

Cons

- Priced according to host
- Cloud recording is a complement to the Basic plan.
- Need Video Conference Codec and (payable) Cloud Connector account to connect

3) Pricing

Zoom provides four types of pricing plans at a starting price of $14.99 / mo/host, including the Basic, Pro, Business, and Enterprise plans. While ezTalks provides three kinds of pricing plans, namely Starter Unlimited, Professional and Business Plans at a lower $12.99 / mo/host starting price. Both Zoom and ezTalks offer free trial options with the chance to enjoy screen sharing and online meetings. It is worth mentioning that ezTalks can be reached by phone call-in, and 100 mins free trial of Webinar is available.

4) User Suggestions

ezTalks users can appreciate the ability to speak in front of the TV easily without being bound to their earphones or setting up a camera.

What's more, along with its program, different useful features can only be found depending on the Internet, which is simple to manage.

Even ezTalks allows each user to hold a meeting either as a group or as a private meeting. There are diverse choices to make.

Yet Zoom's download is small, less than 10 MB in size, earning great customer love. Zoom provides the incorporation of more third parties than ezTalks. It's easy to use, but if you choose to add more participants, compared to other programs, it's a little costly.

5) Performance

These are excellent servers for the simultaneous sharing of documents, images, and videos from anywhere on your computer at any time. Although you cannot be in person (physically) for any situation, you can use stereo audio and 1080p HD video resolution view operation to activate the application online. You may launch a one-click meeting with a specific meeting ID and invite the participants. You can enjoy smooth meeting controls with the help of these two items, such as the ability to mute or dismiss participants, and to "whiteboard" or annotate while sharing the screens. So if you want to add more people or to increase the time limit, you'll cost Zoom more than ezTalks. You can test them with the free trial and compare their performance, respectively.

Bottom Line

Online meetings are accessible, time-saving, and physical sessions are as interactive. Most of the best video conferencing applications can provide you with an efficient Web conference experience that can save time and money. But which solution is stronger, and which is the app for top screen sharing? Computer ezTalks, or Zoom? In fact, the question isn't "Which one is better? "But," What program is right for your budget and needs? "Better software can undoubtedly boost employee productivity, teamwork, and save resources. Therefore, investing in a proper communication platform with a wide variety of features is essential for companies. ezTalks will do anything you want, with great convenience and a lower price for its superior services!

2.6. Cisco Webex Vs. Zoom

Cisco Webex Meetings and Zoom are currently amongst the most popular web conference platforms on the market. All are specialized in web conferences but are part of broader tool suites that can allow users to maintain their web conferencing, Webinar, VoIP, and other communication applications all from one program. Both also have complimentary hardware for using video conferencing equipment in tandem with their web conference features.

Zoom is spread fairly evenly across small businesses, mid-size businesses, and businesses when it comes to the size of their users' businesses. Enterprise buyers use Webex Meetings more frequently. Cisco is a famous company in both the software and hardware sectors, so it would make sense for users of other Cisco products to consider choosing Cisco for their web conference tool as well.

1) Characteristics

Zoom and Webex Meetings are very similar items on the surface, but they both have unique features to consider when deciding between the two.

Webex Meetings could be better suited to larger organizations and businesses hosting a large number of external meetings. Because Webex Meetings can be easily used in conjunction with other Webex communications tools from Cisco, buyers looking to consolidate their web conference, Webinar, and cloud-based phone system tools are the right choice.

The zoom is an excellent match for organizations of all sizes or those in a time of rapid growth or transition. It is built to scale with the needs of your company.

It gives the flexibility to integrate your meetings, webinars, and conference calls online with each other.

It is also an excellent fit for those looking to use their VoIP and team chat software to consolidate their web conferencing software. Reviewers especially enjoy the high quality of Zoom's online audio and video meetings and find their user interface simple to use.

2) Limitations

While Webex Meetings and Zoom are the leaders in applications for web conferencing, both have certain limitations.

Webex Meetings receives praise for the capacity of users to host meetings on multiple types of devices. However, it can be challenging to access and learn how to use some of its more advanced features like interface customization. Reviewers also report that Webex Meetings experiences more occasional lag compared with other web conferencing tools.

Zoom is sometimes praised for its overall ease of use, but its user interface is often a little too sparse, if not quite clunky. In particular, it's "exit meeting" button gets fire from critics because of its position on one's screen and its ability to "escape" when not toggled over. For those who want the most straightforward setups, zoom may not be the right choice too. Although it does have a browser-based client, it does not have the same functionality as the desktop version.

3) Pricing

Webex and Zoom meetings have comparable tariff plans. They both offer similar capabilities in Free Plans. The key difference between the two software offerings is that the Free Plan of Webex Meeting enables users to host meetings of any length, whereas the Zoom caps meeting times to 40 minutes per session.

Webex Meetings next two rates planned for small teams and mid-size teams are cheaper at $13.50 / mo per host, and $17.95 / mo per host, respectively, compared to zoom.

With Zoom, it costs small teams of $14.99 / mo per host and mid-size teams, which is $19.99 / mo per host. These deals build on the integration of the software with other apps and extensions to the use of different networking platforms, including Webinar, VOIP, etc.

Zoom becomes the cheaper option when it comes to their Enterprise plans at $19.99 / mo per host compared to the $26.95 / mo per host at Webex Meetings. This tier allows users to grow through the number of participants they have. Although Webex Meetings allows up to 200 participants, Zoom is increasing that number to 500, and it will enable users to benefit from its webinars and solutions for room systems. Because of this, buyers from larger organizations looking to accept online meetings in all divisions will see greater cost savings with Zoom.

Which One Is For You?

Zoom and Webex Meetings have fairly comparable prices, but if you're on a budget, Webex Meetings will cost significantly less per month, but at the cheaper price, you'll trade 50 fewer participants.

And while Webex Meetings are more commonly used among mid-size firms and businesses, Zoom is more prevalent among small businesses. Consider your budget as well as the average size of online meetings that you wish to host regularly when comparing these two powerhouses.

2.7. BlueJeans Vs. Zoom

Unlike Zoom, BlueJeans also specializes in the video conferencing environment, providing resources such as online video meetings, huddle rooms, and support for events. BlueJeans also offers features for social broadcasting, which enable users to cast content into social media. BlueJeans is a pioneer in its industry, offering consumers from all backgrounds a diverse variety of services and packages.

Meeting Room Products

At transforming the meeting room area, both Zoom and BlueJeans seem to excel. If you are looking for a small huddle-room solution or something more significant, you will find with any of these vendors the immersive video and audio-conferencing services that you need.

Meetings of BlueJeans:

BlueJeans Meetings is an easy, convenient way for companies to access business-grade video calls with Dolby Audio High-Definition support. Users on any mobile device, conference room network or laptop will immediately communicate with customers and coworkers. BlueJeans Meetings also offers services such as:

- One-Click Scheduling: You can add a video call to any Outlook or Google calendar with one button, without entering any code, passwords or conference IDs.

- Screen sharing and collaboration: Immediately share your new documents and video clicks or share the entire screen.

- Dolby Voice Audio: High quality, high-definition sound with automatic suppression of background noise.

- Easy Integrations: Improve efficiency with a range of

Skype for Company, Workplace, and Slack integrations.

- Cloud Sharing and Recording: Capture and exchange audio, video, and documentation meetings.
- Verified security: Ensure a variety of secure deployment options.
- Space compatibility: Users can access Polycom, Cisco, Life-size meetings and a range of other space tech services based on the SIP.

Zoom Meetings:

Described as the leading company for video conferencing and online conferencing, Zoom has created an excellent Meeting Room solution for its clients. According to 2017 surveys, the company currently has a sector-leading net promoter score of 72. The company Zoom Meetings comprises:

- Online meeting services: HD audio and video support with screen sharing and collaboration for up to 500 video participants, apps built-in
- Training services: Co-annotation and white boarding solutions, as well as a measure of attention to keep the participants focused
- Technical support: Facilities for quick start and enter, remote screen control and more
- Integrated scheduling: Zoom operates with a built-in scheduling program for a client, including job addresses, mobile programming and more

Room Products

"Rooms" are evolving as a more common meeting room solution, as companies are searching for ways to integrate anything they need in a conference setting, including white boarding, networking, and video collaboration.

56

Zoom and BlueJeans both provide their own exclusive room service:

BlueJeans Rooms

The BlueJeans Rooms product is designed to help companies transform any business space into a fully immersive video and audio conference room. BlueJeans Rooms allow people to be linked to any SIP conference room network and mobile or desktop users, including the following:

- Wireless screen sharing functions: Display your laptop screen anywhere in the meeting room
- Google and Microsoft Calendar Integration: Set up follow-up meetings to suit the schedule of all
- Universal configuration features: The primary user interface comes with easy-to-read instructions and wrap-up reminders, so no training is required.
- Central management: Customers can monitor any room in their BlueJeans network remotely, and identify problems with a live console.
- Support services: Expand the size of an IT organization with a team of global conference experts from BlueJeans.

Zoom Rooms

Zoom provides a highly flexible and creative room experience based entirely on software, complete with optimized audio features, seamless camera systems, and wireless content sharing solutions. Such features of the Zoom Rooms include:

- Integration with anyone: Via laptop, smartphone and other conference system apps, everyone can access HD video and audio
- Wireless sharing: Dongles and cables are not required; you can easily wirelessly view content from a

smartphone or laptop

- Starting with the one-touch meeting: use voice commands and one-touch meetings to launch scheduled conferences or instant messaging on your calendar system.
- Overview and management: from a single user interface to view and manage your conference rooms
- Native Integration: Zoom provides simple integration of microphones, tablet access, and all-in-one microphone output with Crestron Mercury device

Pricing

The program delivered on a regular subscription basis by Zoom and BlueJeans is close in several respects. After all, both organizations are committed to providing high-performance audio and video conferencing solutions to their customers within a diverse meeting room environment. Of course, one-way consumers can more quickly pick the service that's right for them is to look at the different prices and package packages. Take, for example:

Availability and Prices for BlueJeans:

BlueJeans offers three separate kit and pricing options, including:

1. **Me**: Small business and person network, this program is available at £ 9.99 per host every month, allowing meetings of up to 50 members, connectivity from either computer or mobile device, and unlimited meetings. There is also access to Dolby Audio High Definition.

2. **My Team:** Built for mid-sized companies, this £13.32 kit allows up to 75 members to meet and includes cloud meeting recording, a dashboard command center, and historical meeting analytics. Users can also incorporate HipChat, Skype for Company, and Slack into My Team.

3. **My Company:** Optimized for the business world, My Company provides meetings for up to 100 attendees, along with support for room system schedule, personalized branding apps, and unrestricted cloud reporting. There is also a service for the control and monitoring of live meetings.

Zoom:

One area in which Zoom is different from its competitors is the packaging options. Zoom has a simple "free" version available to consumers, while many other companies do not offer the same option. Packages for the Zoom include:

- Basic
- Pro
- Business
- Enterprise

BlueJeans vs. Zoom: What to choose?

Both Zoom and BlueJeans often get fantastic user feedback, offering a range of similar apps to choose from. Of course, both companies offer a free trial opportunity if you're trying to try something out for free before buying it.

No matter which contender you pick, you're sure to find that your enhanced conference program is improving your company communication and productivity.

Chapter 3: Tips for Getting the Most Out of Zoom Video Conferencing

Zoom video conferencing can be a staple of modern communications, but the technology is still young enough to make room for improvement. A video conference can be either the best thing on Earth or one of the most uncomfortable things you can imagine, depending on how you plan.

Zoom is the best video conferencing solution, but it's just one piece of the video conference experience. To make participants feel as if they meet face-to-face, the entire process needs to be seamless.

You'll need the right hardware and, maybe, a minor shift in the way you use your computer to make your interactions with others come alive. If you are using a tablet or cell phone, hardware options may not have as much versatility as desktop computers, but there are still things you can do to improve your experience. Let's look at the elements required for an excellent video gathering experience:

The following tips will help ensure that you conference in an enjoyable, constructive manner whenever you confer:

3.1. Choose Your Surrounding Carefully

The context which appears in your video is an essential element of video conferencing. The best backgrounds are neutral, and you and what you say do not steal focus away from you. **Fancy posters can look fantastic in private conversations, but they seem very unprofessional and distracting to your viewers.** Consider what a qualified participant would expect and do the same.

3.2. Dress for the Occasion

The dress is another significant aspect. It is better to clothe yourself absolutely – otherwise, as one CEO did, you could unintentionally show boxers underneath the suit and tie. Dress up with an emphasis on convenience, rather than sophistication, when in doubt. Video conferences can be pretty long and the more comfortable you're in your clothes, the more attractive the opportunity.

3.3. Focus on House Furniture

Furniture is essential both when you're just a single participant and when organizing a video conference for a group. The chair and table should be ergonomically set up to enable natural, comfortable seating. In group settings, the focus should be on oval tables rather than the classic, long conference tables.

3.4. Invest in a Good Camera

Healthy hardware is an absolute must in all situations. Cameras that are built-in the laptops are a poor choice for video conferencing because they often ignore the accuracy of the recorded video and audio. Even the cheapest webcam will dramatically outperform those offers, allowing for a trouble-free conference. Ideally, **you're going to want to look at business solutions** designed specifically for video conferencing and delivering superior performance in all aspects.

Webcam doesn't ask you to drop 250 dollars on the most expensive webcam you can find. Many webcams can deliver the professional quality of video that makes Zoom's high-definition and high-quality video quality shine. A 720p (1280 rb720) camera would be adequate for this. To stop choppy footage, get one under this resolution, which can produce at least 20 frames per second. If you want to invest the gas, get one that will shoot up to 30 frames per second.

Get a camera with highly sensitive autofocus and light correction capabilities to counter sudden movements and changes in lighting. It can be annoying to have to change your camera's focus manually, as participants watch your fingers fiddle around the lens.

3.5. Good Lighting is Important

Whatever the camera model you use, it's absolutely important to have good lighting. Poorly lighted spaces are the right way of hampering call quality and affecting your contact with others. Investing in just a few more powerful lights or merely rearranging your workspace is a cheap, easy way to improve the video conference quality without having to spend extra money or effort. Rearranging heavy furniture is also an excellent way to get workplace exercise done!

3.6. The Right Posture

Next are the finer details, such as keeping the proper posture. Slouching is out entirely, but the way you sit may impact the video conference quality. Try to maintain a stance that is upright but comfortable, which will provide excellent back support. **Sitting in the wrong posture for a long period of time brings too much stress** on the lower spine, leading to pain and back problems. Neither will make the conference enjoyable anymore.

3.7. Make Eye Contact

Human beings are social creatures, and one aspect of the intricate network of relationships is posture. A further issue is eye contact. In general, try to stay focused on the partner and aim your camera to make eye contact, or as close as possible to one. This will not only make you look focused and respectful but will also give the conversation a more professional, direct tone.

3.8. Bandwidth Management

Connectivity problems is video conferencing epidemic, but most of them can be traced back to one thing: bandwidth. As stated by lifehacker's and numerous other websites, dial back bandwidth-intensive activities for optimal call quality. Evite downloads such as the plague, limit your visits to resource-intensive websites and try cutting back on multiplayer games for the duration of the conference. Shockingly, the connection is clogged with heavy server traffic.

Tips For Improving Your Internet Connection

In Zoom, the audio or video sometimes gets choppy or distorted. Use the best connection you can to the internet.

1. Wired links are stronger than wireless communications (Wi-Fi, or cellular).

2. Wi-Fi connections are better than cellular connections (3G/4G / LTE).

3. Plan for Zoom meetings ahead, and join Zoom meetings as often as possible from a place where you have a fast, reliable wired Internet connection.

4. When you're not speaking, mute your microphone.

5. When your microphone is turned on, Zoom will devote part of your Internet connection to an audio stream for you, even if you don't speak. Mute your microphone and allow Zoom to use your Internet connection more effectively when you don't need it.

6. Stop video from your camera when you don't need it.

7. If you're doing that with your instructor or moderator, start your video only when you need to show yourself on the webcam, and stop your video when it's not required.

8. Disable video on the HD Webcam.

9. Webcam video broadcasting high definition (HD) requires more bandwidth than non-HD sending. Disabling HD video for other parts of your Zoom meeting will free up more of your Internet connection.

10. Close your computer to other, unneeded applications.

11. Meetings with zoomers will require considerable memory and processing power from your machine. Closing other applications during the session, which you don't need, will make Zoom run smoother.

12. Evite other activities that steal bandwidth.

13. Don't start other bandwidth-intensive activities just before a Zoom meeting, or during that. On your Zoom device – and on other computers and devices that share your Internet connection as much as possible – avoid:

    - **Large Uploads**
    - **Big Uploads**
    - **Video streaming (e.g., Netflix, Hulu, and YouTube)**
    - **Cloud backups (e.g., CrashPlan, Carbonite)**
    - **Synchronizations of cloud files (e.g., OneDrive, Dropbox);**
    - **Other high bandwidth operations**

14. Communicate with your Zoom Meeting instructor or moderator.

15. If a slow one, such as a weak cellular data connection, is the best Internet connection you have for Zoom, let the person or people running your session know in advance.

3.9. Invest in Good Quality Microphones

The type of microphone that you use will impact the ability of other participants to hear from you. Instead of the camera's built-in microphone, you can probably use a headset or clip-on microphone because you don't always remain close to the camera's microphone. If you want people to understand you correctly, choose one that you can hold close to.

You should choose a microphone with an ample range of frequencies. If you buy an excellent microphone of studio-quality, get one with low impedance. 600 ohms (almost) or below is fine because it balances long cables without losing the quality of the audio. Make sure to check if the microphones are vulnerable to radio frequency interference (RFI) at all. You don't want a nearby cell phone during your meetings to generate deafening noises.

To properly set up a standing microphone, point it off from any speakers. Headset microphones should be about an inch away from your nose, and a few centimeters away from your lips corner. Clip-on microphones should sit on top of the chest. Think of the degree at which shirt pockets are typically stitched for comparison—using a Bluetooth microphone, a wired headset, or a clip-on microphone with noise-canceling features and a wide pick-up frequency range for better results with mobile phones.

Other Tips For Enhancing The Audio Quality

Audio efficiency is the most critical aspect of a Zoom meeting's overall performance. Here's how to get the best audio from a conference:

- While your laptop's webcam and built-in mic/speakers can work, a Bluetooth or wired (USB or headphone jack-style) headset can improve the call quality for

66

better results. Or consider combining a Bluetooth speaker (an Amazon Echo or similar device may also use a Bluetooth speaker).

- When you join the Zoom call, you may need to switch your microphone and speaker option, no matter what method you choose. Once you have entered, pick your audio source by clicking on the arrow next to the audio / mute button.
- Mute to reduce background noise, to yourself or others.
- If you're like a coffee shop in a noisy location, just mute when you're not talking.
- If you are holding a conference, and the backgrounds of other participants are loud, tell them politely and ask them to mute or try to silence them.
- If your Internet connection isn't of high quality, you may find that the quality of the audio is suffering.
- Seek to disable video to protect your audio bandwidth over the internet.
- If you notice that your audio quality is starting to suffer, avoid downloading software or doing heavy web browsing too.
- If everything else fails, call in using a cell phone or a landline. You can stay connected to the video and screen sharing web conference.

3.10. Make Recurring Meetings With Saved Settings

Zoom lets you create repeated meetings. You can configure the call settings you want once and have them in there whenever you decide to meet, and you can enter the calls every time using the same URL. Just sign in to the Mobile Zoom app, click the schedule, tap the Repeat option, and pick a recurrence. See Zoom's FAQ on scheduling meetings for more information on scheduling meetings in general and all of the meeting environments.

3.11. Record Calls From Zoom as a Video

Zoom lets you record video phone calls. And you need permission to do so. The host of the meeting would have to require recordings in environments. It is worth testing the settings of your account to ensure recording is allowed before you start.

1. Sign in to your account at Zoom.
2. Tap to view Account Settings / Configurations.
3. Navigate to the Registration tab and click Video Recording.
4. It is worth noting that Zoom administrators will allow recording for all users or groups. There is more guidance here regarding recording settings.
5. To record a meeting with Zoom, you need to choose whether to use the local or Cloud option.
6. Local means that you store the video file on your device or in another storage area yourself. Zoom saves the video for you in cloud storage using Cloud, which is for paid subscribers only. Nevertheless, you need zoom on macOS, Windows, or Linux to capture images. When recording a

meeting and selecting Record to the Cloud, the video, audio, and chat text are recorded in the Zoom cloud.

7. When the call to zoom begins, you will see a choice to record at the bottom of the screen. Clicking that lets you log in the Cloud or locally.

8. If you can't see the recording feature, check your web app settings (under My Meeting Settings) or have your account administrator activate it. You can transfer the recording files to a computer, or stream them from a browser.

9. You can also see during the meeting which participants are recording the meeting, and when the meeting is recorded, it will also be told to those at the meeting. When the call is over, Zoom will turn the recording automatically into a functional MP4 video format.

3.12. Record Zoom Meetings on Mobile

Zoom meetings and calls can be recorded on mobile too. This is done via cloud recordings, however, so you'll need a paid Zoom membership to use this feature. Also notable is the minimal cloud storage, so be careful how many meetings you record when using the mobile app.

Follow these steps to record a call to zoom on mobile:

- Open your mobile app to zoom in.
- Click to join or to open a meeting.
- Tap the three-dot button to the bottom right of the screen
- Click "Save in the cloud" or "Register."
- You will then see a recording icon and the ability to stop or pause recording.

- You can find the recording in the Zoom site's "My Recordings" section when the call is finished.

Where does Zoom save tapes?

Zoom call recordings are transferred to the Zoom folder on your Desktop or Mac while you're recording locally. You can find those at these locations:

PC: C: \User Name\Documents\Zoom

Mac: /Users / Documents / Zoom

By opening the Zoom app and navigating to meetings, you can easily access Zoom recordings. When you see a "registered" tab where you can pick the meeting, you need to either play or open the recording.

Log in to your account and link to the My Recordings page for cloud storage of your Zoom Meetings recordings.

3.13. Virtual backgrounds

If you want to spice up things a bit or whether you don't want anyone to see the disgusting mess of your home on the Zoom call, there's good news as Zoom provides virtual backgrounds. These are the backdrops for your calls, which also include things like space, cityscapes, and views on the ocean.

You can also upload a picture of something you want to customize your context with the Zoom virtual backgrounds. It is available for iPhone as well as desktops.

How to use virtual Windows backgrounds?

- Getting started with virtual Zoom backgrounds is relatively easy. For example, on a Mac or PC, just open your Zoom app, click at the corner on the "Setup" icon, and pick "Virtual Background" from the side menu.

- Zoom has some virtual backgrounds to it. Click on the one you want to be using. Tap on the plus sign above and to the left of the sample backgrounds. If you wish to your background, select a picture from your camera, and then add it.

- You can add a virtual backdrop to a conference, too. Tap the button next to the video on the left-hand side of your Zoom client, select "Choose a virtual background ..." and the same Virtual background page will appear.
- It is recommended to use a green screen and an excellent webcam to get the best results, but a virtual background can also be used without a green screen.

How to use virtual backgrounds for mobile applications?

You can also use virtual backgrounds to zoom in on the camera.

- Login to your account and join a meeting through your phone. Tap the three dots appearing at the bottom of the screen, then click on the menu "more." Tap on "digital backdrop," then pick the context you want to use.

3.14. Take Transcripts

You can also automatically transcribe the audio of a meeting you are recording to the Cloud, as well as recording Zoom meetings. You can edit the transcript as the meeting host, search the transcript text for keywords to access the video at that moment, and post it.

Sign in to the Zoom web portal and navigate to My Meeting Settings to allow the Audio Transcript feature for your use, then go to the Cloud recording option on the Recording tab and verify that setting is available. Should the need be, pick Turn On. If the choice is greyed out, it has either been locked at Group or Account level, and you will have to contact your Zoom administrator.

3.15. Gallery View

For gallery view, depending on your computer, you see up to 49 conference participants at once, rather than the default 25.

You can start or join a meeting using the Zoom Mobile app on Android and iOS. By default, the active speaker view is shown in the Zoom mobile app. You can see a video preview in the bottom-right corner if one or more participants enter the group. You can view the video of up to four participants simultaneously.

Whether you want to show 49 users, you'll need the macOS or Windows Zoom Desktop application. After you've installed the mobile software on your device, you need to go to Settings and select videos to open the video settings tab. Then, allow the "Display up to 49 participants per screen in Gallery View" option.

3.16. Sharing The Screen With Zoom And Using Pause

Did you know you can share not only your screen (smartphone and desktop) but also pause the sharing of your screen? If you don't want your meeting attendees to watch, you mess with your presentation slides, just press Pause Share.

Share and mark on mobile phone

While in the meeting, you can share files directly from your phone, and use the white boarding feature on your phone by writing your finger comments. To annotate while viewing the shared screen for someone else, select View Options from the top of the Zoom window, then select Annotate. A toolbar will appear with all your annotation options-for example, text, draw, arrow, etc.

3.17. Zoom Keyboard Shortcuts

During Zoom Meetings, different shortcut keys can be used to access features or change settings easily. These include a host of things, but our favors are:

Alt+A or Command(affiliated)+Shift+A: Audio mute / unmute

Alt+M or Command(affiliated)+Control+M: Mute / unmute audio for all but the host

Alt+S or Command(affiliated)+Control+S: Screen sharing start

Alt+R or Command(affiliated)+Shift+R: local recording start / stop

Alt+C or Command(affiliated)+Shift+C: Cloud recording start / stop

Alt+P or Command(s)+Shift+P: Recording pause or resume

Alt+F1 or Command(al)+Shift+W: turn to active video meeting view of speakers

3.18. Hide Non-Video Participants

Your screen may get cluttered with participants on a bigger call, which can be distracting, especially if some don't have their cameras on. Hide non-video participants by going to Settings > Video > Meetings and search Hidden non-video participants. Now you're just going to be interrupted by the pets and kids of your colleagues who appear on the screen.

3.19. Don't Worry (Too Much)

Finally, simply worry less is the single best way to improve your video conferencing. Don't think about networking problems, how you feel, how you're going to get off in conversation, or how you're getting ready. It's nice to have some concern, but don't let that overpower you. Video conferencing is, after all, there to allow simpler, natural conversation. Seek to have fun with a shift as weird as it sounds.

Conclusion

Zoom is providing everything you need for sensational video conferencing at all price ranges. The quality of the video you get is excellent, and the audio is clearly coming through too. You can share multiple screens and annotate projects using whiteboard functions. Zoom also lets you connect to any device that suits you – including your smartphone.

Perhaps Zoom's biggest benefit is how accessible that technology is. Setting up a Zoom Meeting is as easy as clicking on an invitation connection to start the app or asking users to install the GUI. There is no need for any mass-provisioning solutions, and the interface on both mobile and desktop devices is lightweight and straightforward.

Zoom also offers super-fast functionality, with audio and video of high quality at every price point.

The free edition of Zoom equips you with the essential resources available to connect remotely with others. Quality is optimum with this method, even for its users who are not paying. It leans more to the budget-friendly side, relative to other applications of its kind — no need to think twice as Zoom is a bang for the buck.

It is one good video conferencing software despite a few hiccups with Zoom. Its ability to provide high-definition audio and video quality is outstanding, even though it needs a stronger link to the internet. The benefits overall outweigh the drawbacks, and Zoom is worth it.

References

Desiderio, L. How to Zoom – Downloading and Installing the Zoom Application prior to your first Zoom Meeting. Retrieved from https://www.bates.edu/helpdesk/2020/03/23/how-to-zoom-downloading-and-installing-the-zoom-application-prior-to-your-first-zoom-meeting/

What Equipment Do I Need To Use Zoom? - University Information Services. Retrieved from https://uis.georgetown.edu/zoom/install/equipment/

How to Set Up a Zoom Meeting. Retrieved from https://www.howtogeek.com/661924/how-to-set-up-a-zoom-meeting/

Google Hangouts vs. Zoom: Which video-chat app is better during quarantine?. Retrieved from https://www.cnet.com/news/google-hangouts-vs-zoom-which-video-chat-app-is-better-during-quarantine/

Zoom vs. Skype: A Comparison of Video Conferencing Platforms. Retrieved from https://www.dgicommunications.com/zoom-vs-skype/

10 Simple Tricks To Improve Your Video Conferencing Experience - Young Upstarts. Retrieved from http://www.youngupstarts.com/2014/05/29/10-simple-tricks-to-improve-your-video-conferencing-experience/

Unify Square. 2020. Microsoft Teams Vs Zoom: Which Platform Is Better For Your Organization. [online] Available at: https://www.unifysquare.com/blog/microsoft-teams-vs-zoom-which-platform-is-better-for-your-organization/amp/.

Made in the USA
Monee, IL
02 September 2020